It is time
to plant
the sacred corn
to honor
the pollen
of letting go
and pray
for the
germination
of a new crop...

Also by Marsie Silvestro

Poetry Books
Feast of Sisterly Trance Formation

CD's of Original Songs
Circling Free
Crossing the Lines
On the Other Side
In Avalon
Moving Through Loss
Meditations with Christine Bavaro

❦

Greeting Cards
Journals
Prayer Flags
Candles
Jewelry

Also published by MoonSong Press

Deep Within the Heart of All Being
Tree Wisdom Messages from the Soul Garden
© 2011 Robin Anasazi

Weaving A Pathway of Light
My Journey with the Ancestors
© 2012 Robin Anasazi

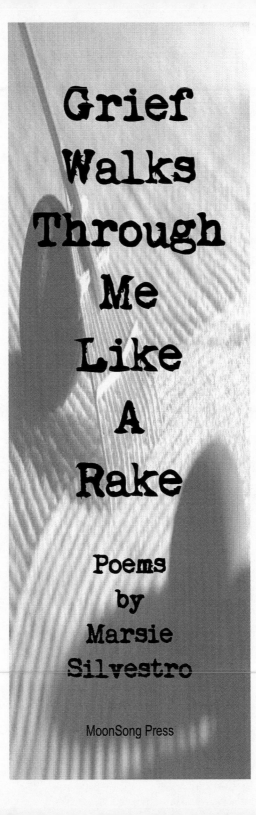

Grief Walks Through Me Like A Rake

Poems
by
Marsie
Silvestro

MoonSong Press

This first edition published by MoonSong Press
Email: marsiemoon@earthlink.net   www.moonsongpress.com

Cover & Book Design © 2013 Marsie Silvestro

Inside Photos: Annie & Robin © 2000 Marsie Silvestro
                 Frost Angels © 2013 Andrea Grillo used with permission
                 Owl in Tree   © 2013 Jason Stemp used with permission

ISBN –13 978-0-615-77943-0

Type Cover: My Underwood
Type Text: Garamond
Printed in Portland, Maine USA

MoonSong Press

For information please contact the publisher at marsiemoon@earthlink.net / 978-290-1029

And to Luna and Ariella, our two cats who also entered into the Light in 2012

*Shape shifting in serenity the Goddess grants me love,
imparts it in my soul through an Angel Being on earth.*

CONTENTS

CONTENTS

ACKNOWLEDGEMENTS

I never expected to write this book but grief walked through me like a rake, and I had no choice but to plant these words in the garden of my healing. I am grateful to those who heard me cultivating my heart and took the time to water me with food, tears, laughter and hugs. The harvest is the pages you see before you.

To Chris Bavaro, Pat Huxley-Cohen and Diane Grant, who helped Robin finish her second book days before she died. I thank you for that and for accompanying me on my spiritual journey through grief. I know you reflectively read these pages in memory of her and blessed them with your inspirational insight.

To Andrea Grillo, Barbara Ferraro, Pat Hussey, Mary Marra, Peg Duddy, Janet Moore, Grace Mattern, Martha Moore, Deb Bertges, Dolly Pomerleau, Rosalie Muschal-Reinhardt, Donna Raycraft, Helen Rousseau, Nancy Long, Lisa LeBlanc, Ellen Secci and Wendy Weise for being my wise women word team. You witnessed my loss, and encouraged me to unfold the rawness of pain and the hopefulness of healing. The mutual companioning of letting go, has raked the deep roots of loss in all of us.

To Sheila Doran-Benyon and Alex Prihoda who offered their beautiful Santa Fe home as a wondrous womb of enormous silence. It permitted me to give birth to my torrential tears and the first poetic pages of this book.

To the Arroyo Hondo Sisterhood of Santa Fe, Sheila, Cameron, Judy, Edna, Annie, Shelly, Rebecca, Kappy and Anita who with dinners, movies, music, walks and artistic presence wrapped comfort around my wounded heart. I am ever grateful to you my Santa Fean Sisters.

To Robin, my partner and Annie, my mom, whose presence will always be a gift. I am ever grateful that I accompanied both of you on this earth. Your light was illuminating and strong. It will never go out nor will I ever be the same for having loved you.

Annie & Robin

PREFACE

In 2012, I lost both my mother, Annie, and my partner, Robin. Their transformative leave-taking into the Light was unique to each, yet the same echoing sonar of loss and grief walks through me like a rake.

Though many people see courage, faith and a sense of peace in me, there are momentous moments at the well of ten-thousand sadnesses which draw tears up a squeaky emotional pulley. Taking steps through the firsts…the first birthdays, the first anniversaries and the first holidays, has placed Zen lessons of complete presence at the feet of my aching heart. Spending Christmas alone for the first time warranted a badge of courage for turning what could have been a pity party into a day of retreat and self -care.

The lifelong strength I absorbed from my mother fumbled, as the loss of her daily calls, her inspiration and cooking support, left me standing in the vast womb of emptiness, suddenly reborn a mid-life orphan. Losing two great and powerful women a few months apart was unthinkable and fi-nite.

As Robin entered deeper into the caverns of ovarian cancer, I entered deeper into a state of suspended animation. I became observer and participant at the same time. Death was surreptitiously entering both our hearts, she who was actually dying, and I the companioned care taker. Simultaneously we were invited to rebirth ourselves and we have.

Finding myself standing in the most sacred of sacred places after Robin died, tears broke open an unexpected reservoir of gratitude revealing that I had truly accompanied an amazing "star being" on earth. As hard as it was to think that she was gone, the immensity of that moment was completely humbling, and I became a tiny speck in the enormous cosmos of transitioning. This unforgettable expansive experience, this anointing of benevolent gratitude, makes her death sacred in my heart.

In the midst of care taking, writing saved my life! It became my "woman cave" where I would go for me and me alone. I didn't have to care or

think about anyone but myself. And ok, I'll admit it; it also put me in a grand state of short-lived denial. Gave me a place to breathe, to free float out of cancer's and Parkinson's view, to reflect and believe that what I wrote evoked the spirits of personal and pliable survival.

The person I was before Robin's and my mom's leave-taking is not the same person who now conduits these poems. I am slowly parachuting back into the atmosphere of reclaiming and reconfiguring life without them. Robin's death was an active and courageous one, my mom's sudden and peaceful, yet both taught me to live fully! It is now my job to integrate and weave the fabric of my colorful evolving existence.

Through years of lived experience, I have come to know that no matter what flavor loss comes in, it hurts, it feels unbearable, and ultimately is the hard rock truth of reality's rawness. We can choose to carry it around our neck like a burdensome rock, or let it break into a thousand pieces freeing acceptance. We never really get over loss; we learn to live with it differently. We slowly liberate ourselves, allowing life and its unexpected gifts to flow in our veins again.

So now, the wild winds of grief constantly transport me to where I need to go and not the other way around. Out of the burning ashes of liquid loss and groveling grief, they have blown the illuminating embers of poetic light onto these pages. Like a freed balloon, they have carried me to places of absolute abandonment and assiduous amazement. What greater healing gift can I ask of these poems than to help me, and those who read them, fly!

Marsie Silvestro
Kennebunk, ME
January 20, 2013

GRIEF WALKS THROUGH ME LIKE A RAKE

Grief
walks through
me
like a rake
picking
at old
snarled roots
stuck deep from
winter's
hard life past.

No harvest
can offer
the fruit
of this
empty moment
nor fertile ground
stand
hands-open
empty
waiting
for new seed.

In the deep
furrow
of lost and found
blessings,
I am told
spring
will
emerge.

FIRSTS

In the
gully
of
loneliness
my feet
sink
sand catching
your name
with every step.

I leave
behind
the forward wind
of firsts
as
I shadow
box
my way
through
our anniversary,
holidays
and blank
calendar boxes
with no
more invitations
to
our life
together.

TWO SOULS FACING THE SAME DIRECTION

Two souls
facing
the same direction
one flying,
filigreed
light
luminescent
last breath
rising,
the other
treading
the muck
of loss,
drowning
loneliness,
while salt water
tears
drip
hollow hugeness
of no
presence.

Simultaneous death,
rebirthing
transformational
change,
intertwining
ethereal
threads,
weave hearts
home
in love's
pure
wholeness.

YOU WERE

You were
my lover,
my partner,
my spiritual companion,
my best friend.

Now
I
name you
hole
in my heart,
space
unfilled,
nowhere
to be found,
reshaped
to catch
wind rattles
shaking
your name
in the vast
vibration
of being
alone.

My guts howl,
bend
to
ricochet echoes
of mournful want,
conjuring memories
of your
precious
breath.

SANTA FE WITHOUT YOU

Santa Fe,
I am
home alone
without you.

Friends
weave me
a blanket
of
comfort
welcoming
me
as half
myself.

Your
absence
is
the
big
sky.

FULL MOON IN SANTA FE

The full moon
paints
the snow
blue.
I know
you
would have
loved
bathing in
its
magic.

I step
out
into the
winter canvas
and feel
the
illuminating
immensity
of the
starry
silken
sky.

It is
large
as the
hole
in my
heart.

A HAZE OF GRIEF

There is
a
haze
of
grief
that comes in
like the
tide,
a malaise
of mindless
motion
that pushes
me
to move
with
automated
steps.

I find
myself
caught
in
time,
lapsing
between
knowing
you are
gone
to
raw
disbelief.

TEARS

Tears
surprise
me
like a
summer
thunderstorm
soaking
my parched
soul.

I am
a
desert
drinking
you.

SILENT NIGHT

The radio
air waves
your voice
on embedded
memories
and
scents
of home made
Christmas cookies
where
my mind's eye
conjures
a dish towel
flung over
a flour spotted
shoulder.

Silent Night,
Holy Night,
escapes from
your circled
shaped mouth
making laughter
dance
across the room
on sugar-coated
syncopated
notes.

Alone
on Christmas,
the vast
silence
of this
night
is wholly
missing you.

GENUFLECTING TO SURRENDER

My knees
bend
dropping
me
to the floor
of grief
where I crawl
on all fours
in a cellar
of
torrential
tears.

I am
at the
mercy
of being
grounded
by
death.

THE PUZZLE OF YOU

Your DNA
is on
every thing
I touch,
your finger prints,
a strand of your hair
the last shirt you wore,
all parts of the
puzzle of you.

Now
I unlock
the
pieces
one
by
one
putting you
in a box
or a bag,
naming you
Good Will,
Shelter,
Friends.

I am falling
apart,
undoing
you
and
me,
a puzzle
with
a missing
piece.

GRATITUDE

Shape-shifting
in
serenity
the
Goddess
grants
me
love,
imparts
it in my
soul,
through
an
Angel
Being
on
earth.

Incarnating
peace,
I open
to the
hallowed
heart-space
of receiving
and
embody
deep
delicious
gratitude.

CROSSING SELF CARE STREET

I am like
a worn out
untied shoe,
ready to
trip
over frayed
and
fractured
laces.

Walking
without
you
can be
hazardous.

So
I learn
to wear
loafers
and cross
the
street
in my
heart.

MOVE AROUND YOU'LL FEEL BETTER

(my mom's favorite saying)

"Move around
you'll feel better"
was your
motto
in
life.

You yourself
were
a merry-go-round
of
love, compassion,
acceptance, humor
and the raising of
your Italian voice
like the
dough
you made
for
pasta, pies
and cookies.

We never expected
you
to leave so fast,
but like
a shooting
star
you were
gone,
moving around
and away
so that
you could
feel
better.

POURING POETRY INTO HEALING

Poetry
pours
out
of
me
like a
broken
water main,
word
gushing
heart
pipeline
to paper.

Thirsty
for a
drink
of
healing,
I anoint
myself
and
let
liquid
loss
flow.

YELLOW STICKIES

You were
the
Queen
of
Yellow Stickies.

They hung out
of books like
bright yellow bananas,
dangled loving affirmations
on frosty mirrors
and
reminded me
which food
I could or could not
touch.

After you died,
I found the one
you carefully hid
under
your bedside
cup.

"I Love You,
Forgive Me
I Forgive You
Thank You
Good-Bye!"

It
stuck
to me
like a
lightening
bolt.

THE LIST ON YOUR CLOSET DOOR

You wanted
an
active dying
so you put
a list on
your closet door
asking us,
"What do you
want me to
come back as?"

Owls, hearts, butterflies,
rainbows and even
a rare Luna moth
were asked
to bring you
back to us.

In Santa Fe
you came,
a Great Horned owl
hooting loudly
on the roof.

I am
glad
the list
helped you
find
the right
costume.

PARKINSON-ISMS

They said you
had Parkinson-isms.

Shuffling feet,
a slightly
shaking hand
and a mind
that sometimes
wandered,
inviting
guests
from another
dimension
to sit at
the kitchen.
table.

Like sex-ism,
class-ism,
race-ism,
hetero-sexism,
the power
to diminish
rose up
in time-lapsed
true-isms,
changing
your charge,
to shake
without the
rattle and roll
you once had
to dance
and rip up the
living room floor.

(continued)

Your sagging shell
was still filled
with fire,
asking me
not to put
the newspaper
on the
clean white
hospital sheets,
a laundry-ism
washed by
laughter,
conceived by
a mother's
familiar
command.

Seven hours
after kissing
you good
night,
in the same
hospital where
I
was born,
I
delivered
you
into death
and
I
began
to
shake.

SLIDING ON THE MISS HER SCALE

I am
sliding
on my own
miss her
scale
from
emotional
earthquakes
to
tear flooding
mudslides,
I am
drowning.

The Rainbow Cross
of friends
comes to my
aide
bringing
survival supplies
of dinners,
laughter
and
tenderness
of
hugs.

Like a
dog whistle,
my heart's
SOS
heard.

DANCING WITH THE STARS

I am
noticing
pictures
of the
two
of
you
together,
framed
on the
fireplace,
hung
on the
wall,
wedged
in old books
and
painted
in my mind.

Who
would
ever think
that
you
would be
a
couple
dancing
with
the
stars.

WE HAD A DREAM

We had a
dream
that one
day
we would
live
in
Santa Fe.

Somewhere
over that
rainbow,
I carry
you
suitcase subtle
as
my new
life
unfolds.

In the
rounded
red clay
of
adobe
houses,
I
feel
your spirit
flying
me
home.

BLESSED BE

Blessed Be...
your lock of hair,
the pile of your clothes
in the corner,
the jar of coconut oil
still on your night table,
the tower of pillows
that held your head,
the cup with the hidden note,
the bills that still come in,
your gym membership
that just ran out,
your car that I sold,
the soup in the freezer
that someone brought,
the colored bottles
lined up on the window sill,
the last card you wrote,
the white and blue handles
in the shower,
the bottle of half used shampoo,
the last book you read,
the tray that carried
your food,
the morphine that helped
you sleep,
the love note sticky
still on the mirror.

Blessed Be
the intermingling
of you
still
in
my life.

SOMETIMES I HITCH HIKE

I am a
foreigner
in
my own
shoes,
walking
holy soled
on an
unexpected
path,
rough terrain,
on the map
of my
becoming.

The high road,
is more scenic,
less bumpy,
serpentine smooth
but sometimes,
I just
hitch hike
and
find myself
a peaceful
passenger
enjoying
the
ride.

IF THE STARS ARE NOT ALIGNED

The icy cold
carries
my
smoke signal
breath
spiraling
through
the glassy
night time sky.

A black
skating rink
of stars
captures my eyes
in
a layback spin
trying to see
if the two of you
are aligned.

If not,
I know
my mother
is the
North Star.

She
is
after all,
a
Leo.

A CHIROPRACTIVE PERSPECTIVE ON HEALING

In
the
pervasive
presence
of
pain
cracking
into
healing,
I
am
adjusting.

ON THE EDGE

I am
a
woman
on
the
edge
of a
new
life.

You
let me
go
like
a balloon,
freed
my
spirit
to fly
with
love's
memories,
a companioned
compass
for the
journey,
so
I dust
off
my hiking
boots
and
pack
my
changed
heart.

GATHERING

I
gather
all the cards
we
ever gave
each other,
we saved
them
for the art
on
the envelopes,
a museum
of
love,
we said.

I
gather
all our earrings,
hanging ornaments
on
framed screens
dangling
sea glass,
shells and
silver shapes,
ear wind
chimes
we said,
to complete
a girl's
outfit.

(continued)

I
gather
all the rocks
the beach
gave us,
gifts
of quiet
walks,
ancient animal
foot prints,
bear medicine,
Quan Yin
we said,
appearing
in our
downward
gaze.

I
gather
paper and pen
and write
your
last day
wishes
and wants,
you said
you never
thought
we'd be talking
about letting go
so early
in our lives.

I
gather
my tears.

MOVE THIS

Move
those flowers
to the left.
Move
that glass
to the right.
Move
those papers
over there.
Pull
the blind
up.
Take
that picture
down.
Slide
that plate
over.
Pile the
pillows
higher.
Rub
my feet.
Straighten
my shoes.

Sister Mary Particulara
appears,
her prayer
to
Our Lady
of
All I Have Left to Control
is
answered.

OH, OH FREEDOM

Oh, Oh
Freedom!
Oh, Oh
Freedom!

We sang that
song
jokingly
as one of us
left
the other
for
a weekend
workshop
away.

Oh, Oh Freedom
I am
song-less
with no
chorus of laugher,
no home coming
of you
on a
hopeful horizon.

The universe's
no joke
imprisons
me.

THE WINGS YOU KNEW YOU HAD

Was there a
door
that
slowly opened
threshold inviting
you to
step
through,
or
did you
jump
onto a
a twisted slide,
arms raised
screaming with
laughter.

Did you wear
sunglasses
as you faced
the beautiful
Light
or were
your eyes
wide open
in
wonderment
as you
floated
peacefully
on the
wings
you always
knew you
had.

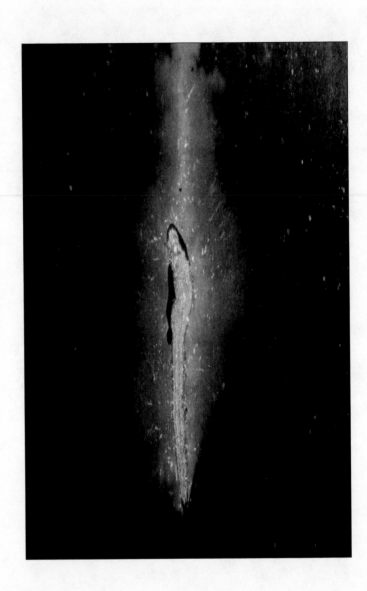

A LUMINOUS LIGHT HOUSE DREAM

I am
walking
water buoyant,
a dreamer's
reflection pool
soothing my
heart's
rippled effect
from
swallowing
too many
salty tears.

Your sensuous
siren's call,
a liquid
luminous
lighthouse,
signals me
to
come upon
the
ancient
ambient
shore.

Floating
on waves
of
having been
loved,
I am
life boat
saved.

SUNDAY MORNINGS

Sunday
mornings
are
the hardest,
hitting me
with fast ball
sadness,
swinging my
life without you,
like a bat
in etch-a-sketch
emptiness.

You always
brought
me breakfast
in bed
and laid
Sunday's tactile
velvety news-printed
eye feast
at my
feet.

I am grateful
for the
spoiling,
it prepares
me to
self care
sauté
my
scrambled
heart.

WHEN WE WERE KIDS

When we were kids
you used to have a pot
of hot chocolate on the stove
steaming our winter homecoming
into the warmth of
a mother's love.

When we were kids
you used to make
candy cane cookies
at Christmas
the favorite request
of our teachers.

When we were kids
you taught us to cook
by the age of eight,
just in case
we needed to survive.

When we were kids
you'd sled ride
ten o'clock at night,
with a sliding sisterhood
of other
neighborhood moms.

When we were kids
we never thought
you who were so active,
would shuffle, fall
and sometimes
forget
we were
your kids.

ANGEL CARDS

Sunday mornings
after breakfast,
our church
was spirit stirred in
a fairy adorned
porcelain bowl
of
angel cards.

One for the day,
one for the week,
two words
of wisdom
carried
two of us
on
feathery wings
of living.

Sunday mornings
after breakfast,
I am not
stirred to
pick an
angel card.

Your
feathery wings
hold me
and that
is all
the
church
I
need.

HANGERS HOLD YOUR SPIRIT

Blouses, Sweaters,
Vests and Coats,
your encapsulated
spirit
hangs like a
dangling participle,
dripping you,
colored
candle wax
down the side
of my memories.

I file
through you
like a revolving
cleaner's rack
rotating the fabric
of
work days,
social events,
weddings,
funerals
and holidays.

Your spirit
is hanging
on a hanger.

This is one
time
I do not
want you
to come
out of
the closet.

HEART OPENING

Release
Relax
Reflect
Rejuvenate
Reprise
Re-group

Breathe
Bend
Believe
Benevolent
Being

Love
Laugh
Live
Linger
Let go

Soft
Sane
Sadness
Solitude
Suddenly

Away
Awash
Aware
Amaze

I
Was
I
Am
I
Become

ON THE HIGHWAY

I am a
word-smithing
guitar playing
musician and composer
lifting cause and courage,
strumming them
home
on notes
I can't
even read.

Tonight
the radio
carries you
4-doored speaker
G clef natural
into the seat
next to me.

An arpeggio of tears
fine tunes me,
joins my voice
in longing harmony
with yours.

I never get
stage fright,
but tonight this
highway
is
a big
Broadway stage
of
mourning.

THE BILLS ARE PILING UP

Like plowed snow,
the bills
are piling up.

Even the mosaics
of
San Vitale
Basilica
cannot compare
to the
impressive array
of table scattered
windowed envelopes,
a saint's
kitschy kitchen art
for the soul.

So I light
a candle
to it's
serendipitous
splendor
and pray
"Couldn't you
think of
a
better way
to get
out
of
paying
your half?"

SUSPENDED IN A RAINBOW

Suspended
in a
rainbow,
I am
prismed,
engulfed by
infinite
colors
carouseling
you
around
the room.

I sit
and
bathe
in this
painted
rhythmic
blessing,
a
textured
remembrance,
of your
spirit
spiraling
Love's
Light.

WHAT DO I DO WITH YOUR UNDERWEAR?

You were very particular
about these sorts
of things
right size,
right brand,
right colors.

You told
me I folded
mine like I
was still
in the
convent.

And now
a drawer
full of your
underwear
has me in
a quandary.

I never
knew
at this age
that I would
find myself
in
such
a
brief
dilemma.

SIMPLIFYING MY LIFE

I am
simplifying
my life.

Death has
a way
of teaching you,
surrendering
your spirit
into
complete
abandonment.

The profoundness
rattles you,
shakes you,
cuts you free
like a
weather beaten
kite
in a
wild wanderlust
wind,
escaping
into an
uncharted
world.

I am
simplifying
my life,
but letting go
of you
was not
my choice.

A MIRACLE BEYOND THE FISH AND LOAVES

I am
getting reports
of you wrapping
your arms around friends
as they wear
your clothes.

You flung open
your closet,
and
invited people
to choose,
to dress themselves
in your
after life energy,
before you
yourself
were
outfit chosen
gone.

You have
multiplied
and divided
the
sum total
of
who you are.

A miracle
beyond
the fish
and loaves.

I AM YOU IN BEING ME

You gave me Life
and the gift
to breathe,
to see,
to walk,
to be of the earth,
to laugh,
to cry,
to think creatively,
to have fun,
to play baseball,
to be caretaker,
to be present in death,
to be fearless,
to use my voice
to speak and sing,
to be a strong woman,
to be compassionate,
to get angry,
to party,
to dress with style,
to cook and bake,
to clean my room,
to give to the poor,
to open my door,
to be fair and just,
to be political,
to respect my elders,
to question,
to get involved in my community,
to be visionary and lead.

I am you
in being me,
and I am
thankful.

YOUR HANDS TOUCHED THE GARLIC

Your hands
touched the garlic.
It was
the incense
of
Sunday morning
sauce,
the holy grail
secret ingredient
to every
thing Italian.

But, you
were our garlic,
the spice
of life mother
who
dressed up
like a clown,
went swimming
clothes and all,
played cards
till morning's light,
a tender teacher,
who taught us
to fly head on
into life.

Your hands
touched the garlic,
kitchen hugs
left us
pungent perfumed
for days.

VEGAN, VEGETARIAN, COCONUT MILK ICE CREAM

You were
careful,
a tight rope
walker
between organic
and selective sugars,
a vegetable
variable
between kale
and collard greens,
a medicine wheel
green shaman,
who raised
plants that
hovered on huge.

But you had
a secret garden,
frozen in the
fridge's frontier
of fabulous,
held in a
ice coated cup
of cardboard,
a cylinder
of chocolate
coconut ice cream,
that you ate
like a mole
tunneling
into
ecstasy.

Even your
morphine
hid itself
in this splendor.

THE ANSWERING MACHINE

You are
immortalized
answering machine
archived
under
L
for loss.

Your welcoming
voice
affirms
a caller's
destination,
a direct
line to us
as a couple,
a company.

Even though
I made
a
copy,
erasing
you
is
like
pulling
the
plug.

ARIELLA

for our cat, Ariella la tu Bella Puss a Nella

Her gray
fuzzy
Persian-Himalayan
fur
was a
prayer blanket
resting daily
in your
lotus position lap.

She was your
temple cat,
your four legged
spiritual
companion
every day waiting
outside
your meditation
room door.

A daily
practice for her
to find
peace
beyond her
cat-lick
upbringing.

No wonder
she howled
the day you died
and
joined you
purrfectly
two months
later.

POETRY AND JUSTICE FOR ALL

upon receiving a book of my friend Bill Callahan's posthumously published poems

Poetry and justice for all
poured out of you
Bill Callahan,
a healing balm
for an aching world,
where
you and I
guitared peace
across the years,
troubadours
of guts and grace,
songsters for the
sisterhood of equality.

When Paradise's garden
called you gracefully home,
you freely gave your sprite spirit,
a courageous culmination
of bread and blood healing
you boisterously bestowed
upon the broken hearted.

In ritual remembrance,
your wife Dolly and I,
simultaneously consecrate
our cosmically colliding
chalices of loss,
pouring
magic medicinal wine
poetry and justice for all,
on you,
my mother,
Robin
and
each other.

THE IMPRINT OF YOUR SHOES

Before my mother died
she kept saying
"Give me my shoes
I want to go home."
Her shoes now
sit enormously empty,
sticking
hide and seek
heels out
from
under her bureau.

Your shoes
ragdoll relax
by the kitchen door,
loaf lazily by our bed,
line up in your closet,
like cans of soup
on a gregarious grocery shelf.

Traveling Shoes
collecting dust particles
of time,
suspended
in deserted space,
stopped suddenly
in tracks,
immortalized.

I never knew
death
had its own
Grauman's Chinese
Theatre.

Grauman's Chinese Theatre where
Hollywood Star's hands and footprints
are imprinted on the sidewalk.

51

YOU AT THE WINDOW

Leaving for
work,
I am
conscious
that you
are not
at the window
waving good-bye,
a daily seventeen year
ritual for
love's departing
ground hugging
road flight.

A shaft of
sunlight
catches the
window on fire,
replacing the
Light of you
who were
Light
for so many.

Sunglasses on
ready to go,
I invite
your
spirit
to join me.

It's your turn
to pay
the toll.

BLAMING THE ANGELS

We would
catch them
on our tongues
even though we
were in our
fifties.

Snow flakes
are feathers
from the
pillow fights of angels,
my mom would say.

She blamed
the angels,
passing her motherly
consolations onto them,
bowling when it
was lightening,
pillow fights
when it snowed.

But we
called
them artists,
painters of carefully
crafted crystals,
ice feather dancers
falling out of the sky.

We only blamed
them once,
lifting
our shovels
in two feet
of snow.

I COME HOME TO AN EMPTY HOUSE

I
come
home
to
an
empty
house
so
filled
with
missing
you.

Sometimes
I
find
it
hard
to
breath.

I
can't
move
without
bumping
into
your
shadow.

YOUR MEDITATION ROOM

Your meditation room
was a vessel
of sacredness,
holding the last
days of you,
a launching pad
for your
hospice journey.

It was your
sanctuary of
sacred strata
layering the
mystical realms,
pouring honey
on the holy
of holies
that encamped
themselves
in you.

Your picture
is still on
your pillow,
I talk to it,
assuring myself
that all the
radiating
luminous threads
you wove,
are tethering
us
to a
lovers'
universe.

MEMORIAL PICTURES IN THE LIVING ROOM

We celebrated you
in a medicine wheel ritual,
remembering
a circle of life
lifted in
the radiant light
you were.

The picture boards,
visually honoring
your living color life,
still rest on
the living room chair.

Your face smiling,
us in Paris,
in New Mexico,
Gloucester,
Hawaii,
a life time
permanently painted
on 4 x 6 glossy
canvases of
laughter and living.

We traveled
a wild
and wondrous
world,
these pictures
prove it.

But now,
what do I do
with all
this evidence?

SYMPATHY CARDS

I am piling
them one by one
on the window seat,
expressions of sadness,
well wishing
stepping stones
for
my journey
into unknown lands
without you.

I
listen to
the vicarious
vibrato of
Sympathy's
Symphony,
words
transporting
notes of
love
and loss.

I am
mesmerized
by the
lives we
have touched
and
by the
crescendo-courage
we have gifted
to so
many.

TIME BREAKS MY SHELL

I am
taking it
a step
and a tear
at a time.

I feel like
I am pulling
a toy train,
cars filled
with
memories,
magic,
and missing,
life times
colliding
on tenuous tracks
to wherever.

Time breaks
my shell,
spills me out
in egg white
slow motion,
makes me
easy over
sunny side up
crazy,
scrambles
me
to unleash
the
yoke
that binds
me to you.

THE FIRST SNOW STORM WITHOUT YOU

We were children
when it snowed
excited about
a day off from work,
time we could read,
cuddle and be
in the
quiet of our love.

We were thankful
for the sparkling beauty
that frosted the trees,
that called the birds
to our birdfeeders,
a color feast of
all feathered saints.

There is a pregnant silence
in storms like these,
an infinite space
within an infinite space,
where Mother Nature wraps
un-worded wind whispers
around your heart.

This is the first
snow storm without you.

A free falling
snow flake
lands on my
eye lash,
you are
a blink
away.

CARETAKING HAS ITS OWN ATMOSPHERIC PRESSURES

They call it
a Nor'easter,
winds shifting
Northeast to North
to West,
off the ocean,
over the land,
a veracious vortex
of
precipitation.

Caretaking
has its own
atmospheric pressures,
a pattern of in-house
companion conditions,
radar and rules
to avoid
the expanding eye
of the storm.

Though
I believed
I was
caretaker
command central,
you made it clear
that you were
still
in
charge.

FEMA
had nothing
on you.

WOMEN HEALERS

You were rolled outside
a wish you had
for your
last day.

Your bed
a sacred subway car,
makes one last stop
beyond the doors
into the
golden sun.

A circular patio
altars you,
where healing
sisters
pour Reiki's
rich energy,
into the
holy frail
chalice you
had become.

Oms and chants
swirled like incense
from hearts
that knew
yours
as tender.

Before my
enlightened eyes,
you are
wholly
anointed
love.

BLESSED ARE YOU

For Robin's Hospice Staff

They waltz
the dance
of angels,
appearing at the
intercession
of your
every need.

Blessed are you
among woman,
compassionate companions,
transporters of transition,
respite repository
of anxiety, courage
gentleness and fear.

Now and at
the hour
of death,
you bring
palliative peace,
attentive anointment,
reverent bathing
of body and soul
leave taking
into
luminous
Light.

Yes, blessed
are you
who have
blessed
so many.

GIFTS

I think of
all the gifts
you gave me
and realize
I am
a department
store
with aisles
of your
teachings
up and down
my heart.

YOU LEARN TO LIVE WITH IT DIFFERENTLY

The pain of
loss never
goes away,
you just learn
to live
with it
differently.

I am
different,
parachuting
back to earth
without you,
finding my own
palpable path again,
creating footprints
in the succulent sand
of new beginnings.

I unearth my life,
lessons of
harvested memories,
fruitful gifts of
a once shared love,
conscious courage
to plant again.

In the formlessness
of what is,
I accept
the blank universal
canvas placed
before me,
hold a new brush,
and make
the first,
of many strokes.

FROM THE OTHER SIDE

You are appearing
in dreams,
white dressed
standing in trees,
guiding friends
to spiritual spas
refreshing their
weary souls.

You are aligning jobs,
synchronizing events
to fall in place,
opening universal
doors to giant
leap out of
your comfort zone
adventures.

You are jumping
off bookshelves
into people's laps,
dancing in snow
creating wind angels
in seven foot drifts.

You are nighttime
star bejeweled,
morning pink sky painting,
gentle breeze gliding,
rooftop owl hooting.

And to think
you thought
you'd get some
rest once
you leaped
to the other side.

GLIDING

I
free
fall
into
a
cavernous
cave
of
creativity
losing
time
and
space
and
a
sense
of
self.

It
helps
me
to
be
surrounded
by
sanctifying
spirits
one
of
whom
you
have
become.

SHAPE-SHIFTING

Something in me
is shape-shifting.
I am putting
you in a different
pocket,
carrying you
in my
backpack of dreams,
planting you
in the
garden of
thank you.

Your presence
is here,
pushing me
to hold on
in a different
way.

Your love is
shape-shifting me,
kicking me
in the ascension
of myself,
repositioning
me
to move
around
so I'll
feel better.

I AM NOT ALONE

I
am
a
woven thread,
a human ley line,
a strand of sorrow,
a link of loss,
an aperture of acceptance,
a heart stretched
across the globe,
lifting a common
cosmic choral refrain.

My words
conjure muses,
paint pictures
of frozen
transformative frames,
pull up emotion's
rotting roots
of perishable pain,
clear my soul's soil
for new seed.

Grief
has wrapped me
in love's leavening shawl,
mingled me
in healing's transposition
of dark into light,
comforted me
in
knowing
I am
not alone.

INTERIOR LANDSCAPE OF HEALING

My interior landscape
has been plowed enough.
It is time to plant
the sacred corn,
to honor
the pollen
of letting go
and pray
for the germination
of a new crop.

I pray the ancestors
will guide me,
send rain blessings
to water my soul,
give me an abundant
harvest to
sustain me
in this,
my new season.

My moccasins
are ready,
the deer has
made her appearance,
the bear has
called my name,
I go into
the woods
vision questing
good medicine,
for my
wide open
heart.

*I wish I could show you when you are lonely or in darkness,
the astonishing Light of your own being.*

Hafiz

Your light was illuminating and strong.
It will never go out nor will I ever be
the same for having loved you!

ABOUT THE AUTHOR

Marsie Silvestro is an internationally known composer, artist and author. Her writings, music and art reflect her many years of empowering women in the areas of personal trance-formation, politics and women's spirituality.

Recognized locally and nationally for her political and justice work, Marsie continues to change lives through her work with survivors of Domestic Abuse and through workshops and retreats for women. Her women's Lead-Her-Ship program, combines creativity with appreciative self inquiry, visionary valuing and connecting celebrations.

This is her first book on grief, but her second book of poetry. Her first book *Feast of Sisterly Trance Formation* was published in 2011. It will soon have a companion ritual book *Feast of Sisterly Trance Portation.* Her fourth book *Fire is My Breath, Blessing is My Blood,* a book of poetic prayers, is in progress and will be released sometime later in the year.

In her quiet moments you will find Marsie collecting sea glass and stones on the beaches of New England or being inspired by the wide open spaces in her beloved Santa Fe, New Mexico.

To order Marsie's books, CD's, creative products or for more information about workshops or retreats (*see page 75*) contact Marsie at MoonSong Press - marsiemoon@earthlink.net or 978-290-1028. www.moonsongpress.com

THANK YOU

Andrea Grillo for the pictures of the frosted angels
that appeared on your kitchen window.

Mary Beth and Jason Stemp for the picture of the owl
who found shelter in your backyard.

Nancy Long for sending me the Hafez quote.

And to the Muses for guiding my heart
to write this book in a month.

WORKSHOPS/RETREATS

Marsie facilitates workshops and retreats in the areas of:

- Healing through Writing
- The Poetry of Grief
- Writing and Painting From Your Source
- The Sacredness of Saying Know
- Woman and Spirituality
- The Muse as Mystic in Writing Music
- Creativity and Ritual in Life's Spaces
- Finding Your G-oddess Spot
- Visionary Lead-Her-Ship

She is also available for individual and group
Spiritual Direction, Retreats and Non-Profit Consulting

For more information:

Marsie Silvestro
marsiemoon@earthlink.net
978-290-1028

REFLECTIONS